Tiny Little Beauty

poems by

Bobbi Buchanan

Finishing Line Press
Georgetown, Kentucky

Tiny Little Beauty

ACKNOWLEDGMENTS

"Anniversary of Mom's Death" was published in *Vine Leaves Literary Journal*
(Jan. 2014, Issue 9) and *The Best of Vine Leaves Literary Journal* 2014.
"Bare Bones" was published in *Kudzu* (Hazard Community and Technical
College, 2014)
"Sycamore Leaf," "Talks to Wildflowers," and "Resurrection" were published in
The James Dickey Review (Fall/Winter 2014).
"Secrets You Know" was published in *Red Wolf Journal* (Spring 2015).
"Orphan's Song" was published in *Still: The Journal* (Winter 2016).

Publisher: Leah Maines

Editor: Christen Kincaid

Cover Art: Austin Whitely

Author Photo: Bobbi Buchanan

Cover Design: Elizabeth Maines

Printed in the USA on acid-free paper.
Order online: www.finishinglinepress.com
also available on amazon.com

Author inquiries and mail orders:
Finishing Line Press
P. O. Box 1626
Georgetown, Kentucky 40324
U. S. A.

Table of Contents

This one's for the students who vanished. The one who read me his poem
on a failed suicide attempt. Another, fresh out of jail,
who needed daycare for the baby girl his ex left behind.
This is for the ones who relapsed, and the ones who broke down.
The ones without transportation or food for the weekend.
Who looked me dead in the eye, and I looked right back as hard
as I could. Sending these words from across the firewalk:
Don't give up.

THE LESSON OF THE SPIDER

The orb weaver's art, strewn
between fencepost and utility pole,
reminds me of the beauty
of purpose and usefulness.
All night she spun
that giant
web.

What
I need to tell you
is this: Find your gift.
Let it consume you. Trust
that others are drawn to that magic.

THE FIRST FALL

The sunburnt maple
sends her love
from the clubhouse
where you smoked
your father's Viceroys,
when boots made you big,
and the hard, dried
blood of scabs felt good
under your fingertips.
Snow would come.
Every winter
would be deeper.

AFTER THE STORM

My neighbor comes out
to clean up leaves and limbs,
pine cones and persimmons
littering his driveway.

Sir, I want to say, go sit on your porch.
Look at the watercolor sky of morning.
See the sunlight on the sycamores?
Every beautiful thing is as it should be.
Blurred. Scattered. Strewn. Golden.

THE SPARROW

I walk out to cricket
song and face full
of sun, clothespin
clamped between
teeth. Nothing
on my mind but this
ministry of damp
socks and shirts.

And you,
little bird.
You
at the top
of that tree.

You
and your feet
in the crown
of a white pine.

Every morning
the earth cracks
open a dream for you.

ORPHAN'S SONG

Blessed are the crooked elms and the bony oaks,
the ragged crowns of cottonwoods;
the runt of the litter and the clumsy beast.

Blessed are the million backyards I have known,
kittens born under muddy porches;
marbles lost in a sandbox, forgotten dolls at the neighbor's house.

Blessed are the bills unopened on a makeshift table,
dishes left soaking in a borrowed sink;
shoes that were always too small for my feet, laces I never learned to tie.

Blessed are the broken, the beaten, the hard of heart;
the faces in the window to my dreams—that other world,
where a mother knows how to braid my hair
and a father carries me on his shoulders,
carries the letters I wrote in his pocket.
Raises me up, lifts me off.
Lets me down.

DAYS CLEAN

This morning you weep
for what's missing, the leaf
you turned over, swept
away in last night's storm.
You ache for lost time, days clean.
follow your grief out the door,
haul your shame to the curb,
shout your hurt to the world.

Take your heart to the river
birch and let her have her way
with you. Get lost in the tangle of her
blades and ribs. Say to yourself,
I'm sorry.
Say, *I love you.*

WHEN YOU ASK ME, "WHERE DO I BEGIN?"

Tell me your dreams, an old story you know.
Tell me how you awoke this morning, eyes
wet with grief.
How willing your heart is to heal.

BARE BONES

Remember the way you drew in this day.
The oak clinging to its dying embers,
the song of a strange new bird. How you
cried in the cold at the wistful howl of a neighbor's dog.
How you wished to be small, and slow, and quiet.
For once, call the dog home.
Open your door. Let him inside.

EPIPHANY OF THE WOODS

Redbuds
and
chestnuts
bare their craggly arms

the wind loves this dance
spinning and twirling
so many partners

The leaves
tell a fortune—
Death can be

beautiful   brilliant   painless

HOW TO PRAY FOR A TROUBLED FRIEND

Lift your eyes to this
clouded day. Fill up
on the beauty of gray.

Breathe in the right
of every wrong.
Watch a gust
take not one, but
every scarlet leaf
from the sweet gum.

Wash your face
with tears.
Remember
every good thing
in the world.
Amen.

FOLLOWING OUR FATHERS
for Barry

One morning you wake up and the dance is over.
The Kipling poem leaves your tongue one last time.
Korea comes back, the flash and boom of Technicolor
nightmares making us into God-fearing men.
And when did our lovers leave us? How did we
get to the top of this hill, to Saint Josaphat's?
Where did our prayers go, offered up through
stained glass and incense, deep in the grottos
of tears we choked back again and again?
And why does the sun insist that we start
this day, alone and old?

RESURRECTION

Before harbinger blooms
and the call of the red-winged
blackbird
           I wished
for that darkness where the woolly worm hides
        to shed myself of myself—
that place where the acorn
falls and takes root.

           I wished for a fire
like yours on a night starred with ash—
        to be born again
Mighty oak, tiger moth.

           I wished for the clean burn
        of new life, like yours—
Big as the sun
        to be born again
in flame.

ANNIVERSARY OF MOM'S DEATH

Traveling back from running errands,
I stopped by the little country cemetery
where they're both buried.
Said my piece. Cried hard. Got back in the truck.
Wiped away tears and makeup.
Breeze cooled my neck, caused me to turn and see
on the cab's back window
two lovely moths with eyespots on their wings
watching me.

EATING BEAUTY

The cottonwoods speak to me, fluttering their petioles,
but I'm busy coveting the boneset at the edge of my neighbors' woods,
the white wisps of a dream; the way the goldenrod there has sprung up,
loosely twined with purple aster, like would-be lovers.
Why does the sight of this move me so?
What is it that my eyes want to eat—or is it my soul?
And why won't I listen to the cottonwoods with their million shiny faces,
their trunks riven with scars, their thick and heavy hearts?

PRAYER TO ORPHEUS

Show me the world through your eyes,
that great calliope in the sky,
the golden lyre in your heaven.

Braid me like grapevine and ivy.
Color me olive.
Call me pretty.

TALKS TO WILDFLOWERS

Purple aster, why do you love me?
Just as I tire
        of this place,
                this path,
                        my feet
You wake me with your electric
 violet magic. I walk
all day with your light in my eyes.

THE MESS OF OUR LOVE

Why try to tidy up
this love affair
for those who
burn the brush
like all the others,
who mow
the stubble of their
lawns, day after day?
I prefer the look of wild
roses to the well-groomed
garden, untended
beds of black-eyed
susans, gangly redbuds
spilling into ravines.

Your face smeared
with sleep, your
hair in brambles.

DEAR NOVEMBER

How does it feel
to wake up half
naked and beautiful,
jewels flung on the earth's
floor, bony branches
jutting out, covered
in starlings?

When I come inside
I'm instantly lonely
for you. I open my
window and breathe
you in. Your starlings
have followed me home.

THE HEART IS A MUSCLE WITH A MIND OF ITS OWN

Yours is a drumbeat
that dreams up a melody
the willful pumping
and the accidental—
sharp, flat, natural.

A heart that thinks
she'll make you
laugh again.

A reflex that masters
a minor key—
the trick of her love.

SO MURDER ME

I am the tramp your mother warned you about—
the liar, the cheater.

I am honeysuckle, forsythia, Virginia creeper.
A threat, a menace,
an angry invader.

I spread across your yard,
choke your trees,
ruin your garden.
But look at me.
Look.
Look hard into these blooms.

My face is a sun of stars.
My eyes are baby
white flowers of the vine
you can't let go.
My body is the musk
of summer after summer
that you can't stop breathing in.

Kill me if you must.
But first, look harder.
I am earth and life and unruly love.
Hands of mud pies,
bare feet in Lost Creek.
Deep down, I am still that dirty little girl.

REGRET

Before you drift
off into that last
long winter, imagine
every sin
coming back to you—

those times you called
your sister a whore, the word
a knot in your throat,

all the stray
dogs you kicked
at the screen door,

every empty beer
can tossed from
the cab of your truck.

Birds you hit,
birds flying back to their nests,
birds flying south.

A MOTHER IN INFAMY

Because I feel myself slipping,
feel myself drowning with her—

We are all drowning. We have filled our pockets in the night and waded
out into the water, hands clamped over mouths, refusing to speak.

She swallowed those rocks, and I love her still, and I will die
without the buoyancy of this love. I will die—

Because I fell from the womb
heavy as tears diving straight to the bottom of a river.

Pebbles shining with mica, shot through with sunlight.
Stones of grief too beautiful, too heavy to bear.

SYCAMORE LEAF

A budding good friend since spring—
Now you are golden and about to fall away from me
        wave your last goodbye, rain down with all the others—

Wait, I say. Come back here and hold my hand—
Close your eyes
Remember your birth
        and the deep, deep green of our summer.

START OVER

At this moment,
the woman who
loves you is folding
your laundry,
searching jeans
pockets for the key
to your salvation:
Arrowhead.
Buckeye.
Beechnut.
Buckshot.

She finds
the blood-and-tear
stained T-shirt,
smooths the seams
as she once smoothed
the top of your head.

One bright day
you will come back to this—
your mother praying you awake,
hunger starting in your belly,
the feeling of joy deep in your bones.

SECRETS YOU KNOW

The sun watches you on that long walk,
drapes light and love across your back.
You want to be the perfect companion
like sweet gum to the warbler.
Swallowtail on goldenrod.
White ash samaras falling to their destiny.
Every tiny little beauty tells you her secret.
What else for that lukewarm heart of yours?
Take that love and burn.

Bobbi Buchanan is the is co-author of *Higher Love: The Miraculous Story of a Family* and author of *Listen: Essays on Living the Good Life*, published by Ginkgo Leaf Press in September 2013, and founding editor of *New Southerner*, an e-zine that focuses on self-sufficiency, environmental stewardship, and local economies. She received the 2007 Emerging Writers Award in Nonfiction from the Southern Women Writers Conference at Berry College. And the 2010 prize in nonfiction from *Still: The Journal* for her essay "In the Woods," which was nominated for a Pushcart Prize.

Her essays and poems have been published in *The New York Times*, *Brain, Child Magazine*, *Sojourners*, *Vine Leaves Literary Journal*, *The Louisville Review*, *The James Dickey Review*, *Kudzu*, *The Pikeville Review*, the *Motif* anthologies *Come What May* (MotesBooks, 2010) and *All the Livelong Day* (MotesBooks, 2011), *Greenprints*, *Literary Mama*, and *Flycatcher*, among other publications. She teaches academic writing part time at Bellarmine University.

A member of the advisory board for the Green River Writers, Bobbi is co-founder of the Homegrown Art, Music & Spoken Word Show, an open-mic and arts exhibition series held bimonthly in Shepherdsville, Ky., and presented in partnership with Color Your City, a substance abuse prevention and recovery charity working to provide local residents the tools they need to create art and outlets for sharing their work.

Bobbi teaches creative writing at the Bullitt County Detention Center as part of Color Your City's Art for Inmates in Recovery Program, which focus on using the arts as a means of rehabilitating substance-abuse offenders—to educate them on the power of art as a mechanism for healing and stress reduction.

Bobbi earned a bachelor's in journalism at the University of Kentucky and an MFA in writing at Spalding University. She lives in Cox's Creek, KY.

www.ingramcontent.com/pod-product-compliance
Lightning Source LLC
LaVergne TN
LVHW021125080426
835510LV00021B/3321